inspiration and
motivation for
WRITERS

Chloe Henderson

INSPIRATION AND MOTIVATION FOR WRITERS

Summersdale Publishers Ltd
46 West Street
Chichester
West Sussex
PO19 1RP
UK

www.summersdale.com

Printed and bound in China

ISBN: 978-1-84953-959-3

Substantial discounts on bulk quantities of Summersdale books are available to corporations, professional associations and other organizations. For details contact Nicky Douglas by telephone: +44 (0) 1243 756902, fax: +44 (0) 1243 786300 or email: nicky@summersdale.com.

To: ....

From: ....

WRITE A BOOK YOU'D LIKE TO
READ. IF YOU WOULDN'T READ IT,
WHY WOULD ANYBODY ELSE?

HILARY MANTEL

The scariest moment is just before you start.

Decide
when in the day
(or night) it best
suits you
to write, and
organize your life
accordingly.

ANDREW MOTION

Make yourself a writing area, no matter how small – a quiet space where it's just you, your pen and a notebook or laptop/computer.

AS SOON AS YOU START
TO PURSUE A DREAM,
YOUR LIFE WAKES UP AND
EVERYTHING HAS MEANING.

BARBARA SHER

Carry a notebook with you at all times, because you never know when inspiration will strike. Jot down conversations you have overheard, make short descriptions of places that you visit and even individual words that you come across. This notebook can be your source of inspiration when you're stuck for ideas. A single word or a daydream could trigger a whole new story!

NO TEARS IN THE WRITER,
NO TEARS IN THE READER.
NO SURPRISE FOR THE WRITER,
NO SURPRISE FOR THE READER.

ROBERT FROST

Never forget the enduring power of a story.

The writing life is **essentially** one of solitary **confinement** – if you can't deal with this you needn't **apply.**

WILL SELF

Learn to enjoy your own company, because good writing requires concentration.

IT IS A DELICIOUS THING TO
WRITE, TO BE NO LONGER
YOURSELF BUT TO MOVE IN
AN ENTIRE UNIVERSE OF
YOUR OWN CREATION.

GUSTAVE FLAUBERT

Create a Pinterest board
to help you visualize
your characters. Find
the following references
in pictures:

- where they live;
- how they dress;
- the color of their hair;
- unusual features;
- their interests
  and foibles.

The more real your
characters appear to you,
the more real they will
be to your readers.

DON'T GO TO THAT BORING, DUSTY COMPUTER WITHOUT SOMETHING IN MIND. AND DON'T MAKE YOUR READER SLOG THROUGH A SCENE IN WHICH LITTLE OR NOTHING HAPPENS.

CHUCK PALAHNIUK

Inspiration is everywhere! Seek it out.

Sometimes
you have to get your
writing
done in spare moments
here **and there.**

J. K. ROWLING

If you lead a busy life, you might feel you don't have time to write your novel, but even the great writers experienced this when they started on the path to becoming full-time novelists. Use spare moments, such as the daily commute or waiting in a line, to jot down ideas or read through a chapter that you have written.

THE PREREQUISITE FOR ME IS TO KEEP MY WELL OF IDEAS FULL. THIS MEANS LIVING AS FULL AND VARIED A LIFE AS POSSIBLE.

MICHAEL MORPURGO

If you're stuck and the writing isn't flowing, do some physical exercise –
go for a walk, dance around the house to some loud music, do some gardening – and you'll soon get the blood flowing, which will give your mind a boost. Some of the most successful writers have a routine that involves physical exercise:

- Kurt Vonnegut always did push-ups to break up his writing routine.
- Haruki Murakami runs around six miles a day.
- Dan Brown takes a break every hour from writing to do push-ups, sit-ups and stretches.

DON'T TELL ME THE MOON IS
SHINING; SHOW ME THE GLINT
OF LIGHT ON BROKEN GLASS.

ANTON CHEKHOV

Remember:

show, don't tell!

One of the
key joys
about being a
writer
is that everyone
seems to do it slightly
differently.

MARCUS SEDGWICK

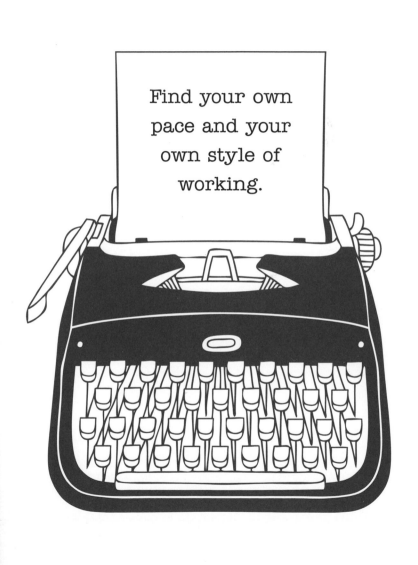

Find your own pace and your own style of working.

GOOD WRITING IS SUPPOSED
TO EVOKE SENSATION IN THE
READER – NOT THE FACT THAT
IT IS RAINING, BUT THE FEELING
OF BEING RAINED UPON.

E. L. DOCTOROW

Try taking part in NaNoWriMo (National Novel Writing Month) in November – where the goal is to write a 50,000-word novel in a month. There is a lot of online support available and, who knows, you might join the ranks of Erin Morgenstern (*The Night Circus*) and Sara Gruen (*Water for Elephants*) and write the beginnings of a best-seller!

LISTEN TO THE CRITICISMS
AND PREFERENCES OF YOUR
TRUSTED 'FIRST READERS'.

ROSE TREMAIN

Take others'
advice on board.

Writing is really **rewriting** – making the story **better,** clearer, **truer.**

ROBERT LIPSYTE

Don't look at your emails until after you have finished writing for the day, because chances are you'll be sidetracked for hours!

REMEMBER: WHEN PEOPLE TELL
YOU SOMETHING'S WRONG OR
DOESN'T WORK FOR THEM, THEY
ARE ALMOST ALWAYS RIGHT.

NEIL GAIMAN

To be a writer, you need to
enjoy your own company,
but break up the writing
time with social things,
too – remember to interact
with your audience! Join a
writers group either online
or in person and learn
from others' experience
and expertise. Henry
Miller put it well when
he said: 'Keep human!
See people, go places,
drink if you feel like it.'

JUST WRITE EVERY DAY OF
YOUR LIFE. READ INTENSELY.
THEN SEE WHAT HAPPENS.

RAY BRADBURY

Enjoy the process of writing and what you learn about yourself along the way.

Proceed
slowly
and take
care.

ANNIE PROULX ON WRITING

Keep your writing time sacred.

MANY WRITERS PLOT THEIR BOOK
FIRST; THEY CAN THEN CLING TO
THIS OUTLINE LIKE A LIFE-RAFT
WHEN THEY VEER OFF COURSE.

ROSE DUTTA

The prospect of writing a book can be daunting, but if you allocate a certain amount of time and give yourself a daily word target – it could be as little as 300 words – the book will soon grow.

THE SECRET OF
GETTING AHEAD IS
GETTING STARTED.

MARK TWAIN

Look **inside** yourself, then **beyond** yourself and see that everyone has a **unique** story to tell – what's **yours?**

I write only
because
there is a voice
within me
that will not
be still.

SYLVIA PLATH

Try freewriting. Empty your head of everyday worries and see what lands on the page.

THE BEST TIME FOR
PLANNING A BOOK IS WHILE
YOU'RE DOING THE DISHES.

AGATHA CHRISTIE

Get your creative juices flowing before you start writing and do some mental warm-ups. Pick an object in the place that you happen to be – it could be your bedroom, the park or a library, for example – and write 50 words to describe that object.

IT IS WITH WORDS AS WITH
SUNBEAMS – THE MORE
THEY ARE CONDENSED, THE
DEEPER THEY BURN.

ROBERT SOUTHEY

Don't overwrite.
Be economical
with your
descriptions.

In the planning stage
of a book, don't plan
the ending.
It has to be earned
by all that will go
before it.

ROSE TREMAIN

To keep the writing exciting, try to plan only a few scenes ahead.

TRUST YOUR READER.
NOT EVERYTHING NEEDS TO BE
EXPLAINED. IF YOU REALLY KNOW
SOMETHING, AND BREATHE LIFE
INTO IT, THEY'LL KNOW IT TOO.

ESTHER FREUD

Sign up to Twitter and follow your favorite authors and publishers. Many of them offer great writing advice, free ARCs (advance review copies) and sneak previews of forthcoming titles. It's also a chance to keep up to date with up-and-coming titles and new authors. One day it could be you!

READ. AS MUCH AS YOU CAN.
AS DEEPLY AND WIDELY
AND NOURISHINGLY AND
IRRITATINGLY AS YOU CAN.

A. L. KENNEDY

Reading all kinds of genres and styles will feed your vocabulary and make you more discerning when assessing your own work.

I admire
anybody
who has the
guts to write
anything at all.

E. B. WHITE

Don't forget to pat yourself
on the back every so often!

ONE MUST BE DRENCHED IN
WORDS... TO HAVE THE RIGHT
ONES FORM THEMSELVES
INTO THE PROPER PATTERN
AT THE RIGHT MOMENT.

HART CRANE

If you have an idea just before going to bed, write it down or text/email it to yourself – because you won't remember it in the morning! If J. K. Rowling hadn't written down the daydream that she had on a long train journey, Harry Potter would never have seen the light of day.

IT'S DOUBTFUL THAT ANYONE
WITH AN INTERNET CONNECTION
AT HIS WORKPLACE IS
WRITING GOOD FICTION.

JONATHAN FRANZEN

Always **aim** to write your **best** **possible** work.

The moment **you can see** any well-planned surprise, chances are, so will your sophisticated reader.

CHUCK PALAHNIUK

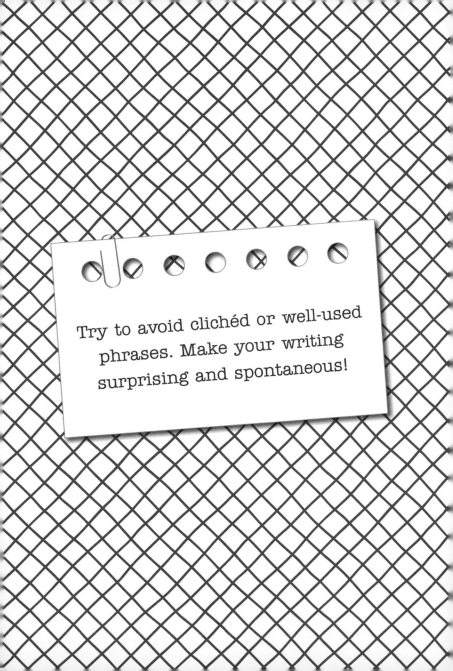

Try to avoid clichéd or well-used phrases. Make your writing surprising and spontaneous!

IF YOU WANT TO WRITE,
YOU CAN. FEAR STOPS MOST
PEOPLE FROM WRITING,
NOT LACK OF TALENT,
WHATEVER THAT IS.

RICHARD RHODES

If you're suffering from writer's block midway through the book, go back and read earlier sections and look for characters and scenes that you could reintroduce/revisit. Better still, take time away from it and work on something else. Many authors have more than one project on the go, partly because it helps them to return to a project with fresh eyes.

I'VE FOUND IT HELPFUL TO
SPEND TIME WITH MY WRITING
PROJECT LIKE IT IS A PERSON
RATHER THAN A THING.

GILMORE TAMNY

Dream your idea into being – don't force it.

Don't hold
on to poor work. If
it was bad
when it went in the
drawer it will be
just as bad
when it comes out.

JEANETTE WINTERSON

Try to explain the basic concept
of your book in a nutshell
to a trusted friend – if you
struggle to do this, then the
idea needs more thought.

KEEP YOUR EXCLAMATION
POINTS UNDER CONTROL.

ELMORE LEONARD

As is the case with anything that requires hard work, the more you do it the better you will become. Write as often as possible, and don't feel you need to carry on from where you left off – you could write a scene that appears later; then you have the exciting puzzle of how to get from where you are to that scene!

IF I GET STUCK I GO FOR A
WALK OR IF I DON'T HAVE MUCH
TIME, I WASH MY HAIR – IT
SEEMS TO WAKE MY BRAIN UP!

ANDREW MOTION

When the going gets tough – the tough keep going!

[It's] better to
write something
imperfect
that you could
improve on
later than to stare at
a piece of paper (or a
screen) waiting for
'the muse'
to inspire you.

DEBORAH NAM-KRANE

Allow yourself to make mistakes.

WHEN AN IDEA COMES,
SPEND SILENT TIME WITH
IT. REMEMBER KEATS'S IDEA
OF NEGATIVE CAPABILITY
AND KIPLING'S ADVICE TO
'DRIFT, WAIT AND OBEY'.

ROSE TREMAIN

Practice writing on all different types of subject and in different formats:

- Offer to write local newspaper articles
- Create a blog about your life or love of writing
- Write daily tweets
- Compose letters to national newspapers on hot subjects
- Write a piece for a magazine on a subject that you are passionate about

It all counts as experience, which will make you a better writer.

THERE ARE NO LAWS FOR THE
NOVEL. THERE NEVER HAVE
BEEN, NOR CAN THERE EVER BE.

DORIS LESSING

Make your own rules and stick to them.

Be your own
editor/critic.
Sympathetic but
merciless!

JOYCE CAROL OATES

Every scene and dialogue exchange must have a purpose; nothing should be there just to make up the word count.

THERE ARE THREE RULES
FOR WRITING A NOVEL.
UNFORTUNATELY, NO ONE
KNOWS WHAT THEY ARE.

W. SOMERSET MAUGHAM

If you have a brilliant idea for a piece of writing, don't immediately assume that it would work as a novel; it might be better suited as a short story or play.

DON'T PANIC. MIDWAY THROUGH
WRITING A NOVEL, I HAVE
REGULARLY EXPERIENCED
MOMENTS OF BOWEL-
CURDLING TERROR, AS I
CONTEMPLATE THE DRIVEL
ON THE SCREEN BEFORE ME.

SARAH WATERS

Even the **great writers** admit to poor **first** drafts – so you're in **good** company!

You don't write
because
you want to say
something,
you write because
you've got
something to say.

F. SCOTT FITZGERALD

Write with confidence, because your opinions count.

THE FIRST DRAFT
OF ANYTHING IS SH*T.

ERNEST HEMINGWAY

Use the track change
option in the review bar
and add comments as you
read through your drafts,
much the same as an
editor would. It helps to
see your thought processes
on the page and you might
decide that something you
had discounted should
be reinstated after all.

ONE WRITES OUT OF ONE THING
ONLY – ONE'S OWN EXPERIENCE.

JAMES BALDWIN

Use your own **experiences** — both **good** and **bad** — as fuel for your **writing.**

I was working on
the proofs
of one of my poems
all the morning
and took out
a comma. In the
afternoon I put it
back again.

OSCAR WILDE

Use an app to determine your Internet usage as a means of trying to cut down the amount of time you spend online.

NEVER STOP WHEN
YOU ARE STUCK.

JEANETTE WINTERSON

Take your cue from
Vladimir Nabokov, who
wrote on index cards,
enabling him to draft his
books out of sequence
and arrange the order
as he saw fit. It can be
quite boring to rigidly
follow a chapter plan, so
write a synopsis of each
chapter on an index card
and then shuffle them – it
might provide the twists
and turns that you need
to make your book into
a real page-turner.

TED HUGHES GAVE ME THIS
ADVICE AND IT WORKS
WONDERS: RECORD MOMENTS,
FLEETING IMPRESSIONS,
OVERHEARD DIALOGUE,
YOUR OWN SADNESSES AND
BEWILDERMENTS AND JOYS.

MICHAEL MORPURGO

Scrimp on punctuation, unless you're writing about the merits of a household product!

Read it aloud to **yourself** because that's the only way to be sure **the rhythms** of the sentences are OK.

DIANA ATHILL

Listen to the voices in your work – do they sound natural or stilted?

WE ARE ALL APPRENTICES
IN A CRAFT WHERE NO ONE
EVER BECOMES A MASTER.

ERNEST HEMINGWAY

Form a group of trusted
readers of all ages – people
whose opinions you value
– and ask for constructive
feedback. If you're not
sure if some of your
dialogue works, get a few
people together and read
it aloud. You might acquire
some good ad-libs, too!

TRY TO READ YOUR OWN
WORK AS A STRANGER WOULD
READ IT, OR EVEN BETTER,
AS AN ENEMY WOULD.

ZADIE SMITH

Be **objective** when reading your **work** – imagine you're **reading** someone else's **words**.

Writing is
not a job
description. A
great deal of
it is luck.

MARGARET ATWOOD

Like life, your characters will need to go through highs and lows in order to appear as real as possible to the reader, and so that the reader will root for them and be interested enough to know what happens to them.

IN A WRITER THERE MUST
ALWAYS BE TWO PEOPLE – THE
WRITER AND THE CRITIC.

LEO TOLSTOY

Break routine once in a
while and surprise yourself
by doing a new activity
or exploring somewhere
new. People-watching
can be very inspiring
to a writer. Imagine the
stories people have to tell,
where they are going and
what their dreams are.

I WRITE ENTIRELY TO FIND
OUT WHAT I'M THINKING,
WHAT I'M LOOKING AT, WHAT
I SEE AND WHAT IT MEANS.

JOAN DIDION

Enjoy the process
of writing and
what you **learn**
about yourself.

Start telling the
stories
that only you
can tell, because
there'll always be
better...
and...
smarter writers
than you...
but you are the
only you.

NEIL GAIMAN

Keep a diary, but make it literary – highlight your experiences, both good and bad, and keep them alive on the page.

FORGET ALL THE RULES.
FORGET ABOUT BEING PUBLISHED.
WRITE FOR YOURSELF AND
CELEBRATE WRITING.

MELINDA HAYNES

One way to jump-start your writing each day is to finish mid-sentence the previous day. This is a common trick used by writers as the first few words should be easy to find, then before you know it you're writing again!

YOU CAN'T WAIT FOR
INSPIRATION. YOU HAVE TO
GO AFTER IT WITH A CLUB.

JACK LONDON

Look for **inspiration** in your own work — **seek** out small clues in your writing that you can **develop** into bigger themes.

Increase
your word power.
Words are the raw
material
of our craft.

P. D. JAMES